Original title:
Tides of Wonder

Copyright © 2025 Creative Arts Management OÜ
All rights reserved.

Author: Eleanor Prescott
ISBN HARDBACK: 978-1-80587-252-8
ISBN PAPERBACK: 978-1-80587-722-6

## The Drift of Time

In a boat made of bubble gum,
I float on waves, oh what a hum!
The clock is ticking, but who's to care?
With seagulls dancing in salty air.

A crab snaps jokes, oh what a tease,
While dolphins leap with such great ease.
The sun's a jester, a blazing fool,
Splashing colors in a liquid pool.

**A Whisper from the Abyss**

Beneath the waves, a fish does sing,
With fins that twirl like a disco king.
He tells of treasure, or maybe cheese,
In a world where anything can please.

The octopus wraps up his best stand-up,
Throwing ink like a messy cup.
I laugh so hard, I nearly float,
Turning seaweed into a danceboat.

**Transient Joys at Sunset**

As the sun dips low, it winks at me,
A playful spark above the sea.
Clouds giggle like kids in a rush,
Painting skies in a vibrant hush.

Crabs in bowties slide to the shore,
Telling tales of the ocean's lore.
With laughter echoing through the breeze,
At sunset's party, we dance with ease.

## **Unraveled Dreams**

In a world where mermaids sip on tea,
They gossip 'bout fish as silly as me.
A turtle does yoga, oh what a sight,
While sea cucumbers giggle in delight.

Stars fall like confetti, a wild parade,
Where each one's a wish that's quickly made.
Under the moon, we spin a tale,
Of laughter, dreams, and a utopian whale.

## A Symphony of Shores

Waves crash with a giggle,
Seagulls dance in the air,
A crab wearing shoes, oh so brittle,
Scuttles away without a care.

Shells sing songs of the deep,
While seaweed does a twirl,
A dolphin makes a playful leap,
And gives the waves a whirl.

Sandcastles start to sway,
As the tide plays peek-a-boo,
Children shout in joyful play,
While the sand gets stuck like glue.

Even the starfish has flair,
Waving in the ocean's breeze,
All the fish stop and stare,
At the underwater knees.

## **Liquid Horizons**

The ocean wears a silly hat,
Made of foam and sun-kissed dreams,
Fish joke about a sleepy cat,
Who snoozes under moonlight beams.

Mermaids swim with silly glee,
Trading tales of lost high tide,
Squids giggle beneath the sea,
As they take a jolly ride.

The horizon winks at us all,
Making shapes with every swell,
While dolphins play a beach ball,
Their laughter rings like a bell.

Jellyfish dance, oh what a sight,
In costumes of jelly and light,
A party of glittering delight,
As day turns into night.

## Enchantment of the Abyss

In the deep where secrets dwell,
Fish wear glasses to read books,
A clam sings a bubbly shell,
While octopuses share their looks.

The seaweed sways, a green ballet,
As crabs put on a talent show,
With a pinch, they dance away,
Before the waves tell them to go.

A treasure chest holds a joke,
Filled with pearls and funny hats,
While fish are tickled, and they croak,
Under the watch of spiny spats.

Mermaids giggle at the sight,
Telling tales of ancient lore,
In this underwater delight,
Where laughter is never a bore.

## Horizon's Melody

Under the sun's bright charm,
The gulls tell tales of the tide,
Every wave has a kind of calm,
And secrets that the sea does hide.

Sea turtles ride on a wave's back,
Wearing shades and looking cool,
While the fish form a rhythmic pack,
In an underwater swimming school.

A lighthouse winks with a grin,
Sharing wisdom of frothy seas,
As barnacles join in the din,
Creating a symphony with ease.

Every splash is a burst of cheer,
As the ocean plays its song,
With the horizon always near,
Inviting all to sing along.

## Whispers of the Moonlit Waves

The moonlight dances, oh so bright,
With jellyfish having quite the fright.
They wiggle and jiggle, what a sight,
In the nighttime sea, they party all night.

A crab in a top hat takes the lead,
While seahorses gossip about the seaweed.
They say, 'Did you hear? The starfish can read!'
And giggle away while they plant their seed.

## Secrets Beneath the Surface

A clam kept secrets, oh so rare,
With pearls of wisdom hidden with care.
But when it sneezed, oh, the fish would stare,
'Is that a moat or a friendly air?'

The octopus boasts, 'I can juggle well!'
With balls made of shells, they start to swell.
But who knew a splash could be such a tell?
A fishy giggle, 'That's stinky, farewell!'

## Celestial Currents Dance

Stars twinkle eager to join the fray,
As whales put on shows, hip hip hooray!
With flips and splashes, they sashay,
While the crabs cheer loud, 'Hippo birthday!'

A dolphin decides to sing a tune,
While turtles are rapping, oh what a boon!
They throw a party under the moon,
And squids perform science at high noon!

## The Poetry of Endless Shores

Upon the sands, the seagulls squawk,
While crabs engage in a moonlit talk.
They chase the waves like a silly flock,
'Time for our dance, let's take stock!'

A sandcastle built with great delight,
But then a wave came—oh, what a fright!
The castle collapsed, oh, what a sight,
Yet the laughter echoed all through the night!

## A Wanderer's Bay

In a bay where sailors jest,
Fish wear hats and pirates rest.
The seagulls gossip, full of sass,
While crabs do the conga on the grass.

Waves come in with silly tricks,
Tickling toes as laughter clicks.
A splash, a laugh, a playful chat,
Even the dolphins wear a hat.

Sandcastles lean, their towers fall,
A lemonade stand, the best of all!
Sharks with shades, they chill and chill,
While octopuses paint with thrill.

As sunsets glow, the shores delight,
With fireflies dancing into the night.
Every wave a tale it spins,
At wanderer's bay, the fun begins!

## **Pebbles Underfoot**

Stumbling over pebbles round,
Each one tells tales of a clown found.
One says, 'I've been on a shoe!'
Another whispers, 'I'm lost too!'

A pebble plops, then rolls away,
'Come back!' the worn flip-flops say.
They giggle as they trip and fall,
These pebbles know it all, after all.

Shells sing songs of waves gone by,
While the wind laughs, oh me, oh my!
Groups of stones form a party line,
Invite some sand, and all's just fine!

Windy days bring tales anew,
Of fish on bicycles, oh who knew?
In this jumbled, bumpy fun,
Pebbles dance till day is done!

## The Forgotten Lagoon

In a lagoon, quite lost in time,
Where frogs hold court and sing in rhyme.
A hippo dons a bright pink hat,
While an old turtle plays with a spat.

The water sparkles, a wobbly dance,
An otter spins in a silly prance.
Mysterious fish pull off their tricks,
As lily pads host their comedy flicks.

Forgetful ducks waddle in line,
Complaining 'bout the lack of sunshine.
A gator slips on a slippery log,
In this merry place where wonders jog.

Bubbles burst with giggles bright,
As fireflies join the monstrous night.
In the lagoon, the laughter rings,
Where even the reeds wear rainbow wings!

**Basin of Reverie**

In the basin where daydreams play,
Fish wear shoes, doing ballet.
The reeds sway like they're in a band,
A turtle smiles, spinning on sand.

Clouds drift low, taking a peek,
Wishing for fun, so cheeky, so sleek.
Frogs throw parties, quite a delight,
With bugs for snacks all through the night.

Mirror lakes hold a funny view,
Reflections dance, making things new.
A dragonfly sings tunes so sweet,
While mud pies form beneath little feet.

Stars twinkle, joining the spree,
In the basin's giggly symphony.
Each wave a wink from dreams so bright,
In this happy place where hearts take flight!

## A Fluid Reverie

The ocean waves dance with glee,
As crabs do the cha-cha, can't you see?
A fish with a hat rides on by,
While seagulls sing karaoke in the sky.

Starfish drinking tea, oh what a sight,
Mermaids lost in a bubble fight.
The dolphins are busy crafting a tune,
And octopuses juggle beneath the moon.

A whale croons an off-key song,
While seaweed sways, oh so wrong.
A sandcastle knight with a fierce plastic sword,
Defends his realm from a beach ball horde.

With flip-flops slapping and laughter galore,
The shoreline's a stage we can't ignore.
In this salty circus, we all play a part,
For humor flows freely, straight from the heart.

## Whispering Sands

Grains of sand giggle as they fall,
They tickle your toes, a playful call.
The dunes share secrets in a breeze,
While flip-flops abandon their owners with ease.

A crab in a shell, wearing cool shades,
Struts on the beach where the sunscreen parades.
Seashells whisper gossip, oh what a scene,
About the clam who flaunted his bling so keen.

Beach umbrellas wrestling in the air,
A picnic blanket fights with a rogue seagull's flair.
Sunburned surfers hang ten in style,
Wooing the waves with each slap and a smile.

But don't be too loud, the sandman will hear,
And he'll come to collect for your summer cheer.
With a wink and a grin, he'll charge you a laugh,
For fun by the shore is a priceless draft.

## **The Colors of Dusk**

As the sun dips low, the sky turns to paint,
Clouds brush pink swirls, a magic quaint.
Seagulls dressed in twilight's thin lace,
Ballet dance through a playful space.

The crickets are tuning their tiny strings,
While fireflies twinkle, like little bling.
A lobster in sunglasses is sippin' a drink,
As the world dons the color of ink.

Paddle boats laughing in a swirling swirl,
Splashing water that makes everyone twirl.
The stars pop out, one by one,
While bunnies in goggles watch the fun.

With shadows growing long, the day takes a bow,
Nature's comedy show is underway now.
So grab a beach towel, settle in close,
For night brings a giggle, we can't help but boast.

## Songs of the Seafoam

The seafoam flops and giggles along,
Like a chubby kid who can't help but throng.
Frothy whispers sing to the shore,
Tickling toes, always wanting more.

Fish in tuxedos waltz with delight,
While logs in the waves join the merry sight.
Starfish applaud with their fancy deckhands,
While jellyfish twirl in their bubble bands.

A clam's little party in a shell so chic,
Inviting the tide for a dance on the peak.
But wait! The tide slips, and he's lost in the froth,
Oh, siren of shells, hope you're not upset, broths!

Shells clink together like a wild night out,
As pearls share stories none would doubt.
In the whimsical world of briny streams,
The laughter of foam fills our wacky dreams.

## The Great Escape

Two crabs plotted a great escape,
Their plan was quite silly, no cape.
They danced on the sand,
With a bucket in hand,
But forgot they were stuck on a tape.

A fish jumped in and gave a cheer,
Said, "Boys, can you swim? Oh dear!"
They floundered about,
With a laugh and a shout,
As seagulls just watched from the pier.

They built a huge raft made of shells,
But it sank like a ton of old bells.
With a splash and a crash,
They made quite a splash,
And returned to their homes with great yells.

Now crabs tell tales of the sea,
Of escapes that were never to be,
With giggles and grins,
And laughter that spins,
In the sand where they dream to be free.

## Ocean's Canvas

The waves rolled in with a splash,
As sandcastles began to clash.
Seagulls took flight,
In a funny sight,
As the tide made a sneaky dash.

One kid built a tower so great,
While another just tried to create,
A moat full of fish,
For his birthday wish,
But they swam away, oh what fate!

Colors painted on seashells bright,
A masterpiece shimmering in light.
But a wave came too near,
And with a loud cheer,
The ocean claimed it without a fight.

So we laugh at the art of the shore,
Where nature's the author, for sure.
With brushes of foam,
And a splash instead of comb,
Life is a canvas to explore.

## Sailors of Solitude

Two sailors sat under the moon,
With their ship, they sang a strange tune.
They joked of the sea,
And their cups of cold tea,
While dolphins danced in the lagoon.

One said, "I'm the captain, you see!"
The other replied, "Oh, let it be!"
But the wind with a gust,
Made their ship lose its trust,
And they sailed out far to the spree.

With a parrot who squawked out of turn,
And a barrel of fish they would churn,
They laughed at the plight,
As they floated all night,
In a boat that just wanted to learn.

They drifted off to lands unseen,
Where marshmallow clouds gleamed and green.
With giggles and glee,
In the vast, endless sea,
They found solitude, simple and keen.

## Legends of the Marina

In a marina where boats love to play,
Lived a shark who was scared of the bay.
He shivered and shook,
From the glance of a hook,
Claiming, "I'm more of a couch fish today!"

A lobster wore shades, looking cool,
And declared he was king of the pool.
But a wave took a swipe,
Sending all in a hype,
As the shadows revealed a great duel!

Anglerfish proudly flicked their tails,
Sharing tales that could fill up the gales.
With each humorous prank,
And a swim in the tank,
They spun yarns that could fill up the trails.

Now legends grow wild by the tide,
Of antics where sea creatures bide.
For laughter and fun,
Beneath the warm sun,
Are the treasures that float with great pride.

## The Allure of Untamed Waters

Jumping fish and tales so grand,
They flip like gymnasts in the sand.
Seagulls squawking, oh what a sight,
They'll steal your chips, then take flight!

The waves are laughing, can you hear?
They're telling jokes to those who steer.
A boat that wobbles, like a clown,
Sinks without warning, then spins around!

Shells that whisper, secrets old,
A pirate's treasure? Just a mold!
Crabs in tuxedos, dance with flair,
Pinch your toe, then strike a pose in air!

Sunsets chuckle in hues so bright,
Painting skies with colors that excite.
So come and laugh, with maritime cheer,
Life's lovely circus, let's all be near.

## Fables on the Breeze

The wind is gossiping, can't you tell?
It shares the stories of sea and shell.
Tickling the sails with a playful tease,
Singing ballads carried on the breeze.

Mermaids tangled in seaweed hair,
Argue over who got sunburnt where.
With fishy friends, they laugh and play,
While dolphins join the grand ballet.

A crab wears sunglasses, grim and cool,
Teaching young fish, all the right rules.
Watch out for waves, they'll quack and splash,
Tripping the surfers with a mischievous crash!

With winds that dance and waves that rhyme,
Life's full of giggles, just in good time.
So hold your hat, or it may fly,
Join the fun where we wave goodbye!

## **Morning Mist on the Bay**

Morning mist wraps like a hoot,
Where boats are pondering, in silly pursuit.
Coffee spills on a fisherman's hat,
As gulls plot mischief, all sleek and fat.

The sunrise paints a pancake sky,
While silly seals wave, oh my, oh my!
They juggle fish in a slippery spree,
Leaving the fisherman grumbling, 'Woe is me!'

One boat floats backward, what a sight,
While old Bob bumbles, losing his fight.
"Who needs a compass?" he shouts with glee,
Just follow those gulls, and hope for the sea!

As morning winks with a cheeky grin,
And the waves laugh softly, inviting in,
Join this folly, let's frolic and play,
In the morning mist, we'll dance all day!

## **Enigma by the Shore**

At the shore, where shadows tease,
Waves wagging tongues like cheeky bees.
Who stole my flip-flops? They run with flair,
Paddling off with not a care!

A pirate's map, full of doodles and squiggles,
Leads to a treasure of jelly-filled giggles.
"Arrr!" yells the captain with a toothy smirk,
While his crew trips over their own hard work.

Sandcastles smile with frosting on top,
And crabs marching proudly, never stop.
Yet the tide comes in, cracking the joke,
As towers tumble, like an old oak's smoke.

So come join me, at this puzzling plot,
Where nonsense reigns and smiles are caught.
Life's a riddle, lost and found,
By the shore, let's gather round!

## The Harmony of Sea and Sky

The fish dance like they're on air,
Seagulls play tag, without a care.
The waves tickle rocks with a giggle,
While sailors stumble in a wiggle.

Balloons float from kids on the shore,
Chasing the dog who wants to explore.
A crab serves tea with a fancy hat,
'Would you like sugar, or maybe a rat?'

The sun sneezes glitter, oh what a sight,
Sunburned tourists, a comical plight.
Shiny sunblock on the nose so long,
They leave the beach, singing a song.

As the day ends, they wave goodnight,
Stars perform in the velvet light.
In this place, laughter fills the air,
Where the ocean chuckles without a care.

## Mirage of the Sapphire Sea

In the distance, a boat made of cheese,
Sails blown gently by a soft breeze.
The captain's a parrot, bold and spry,
He squawks out orders and parties high.

Mermaids try to sell seashells for free,
While dolphins juggle just for glee.
A crab in a tux, he dances with flair,
Slick moves that'll make you stop and stare.

The sun dips low, and shadows grow tall,
A wave of laughter, the best of all.
The fish wear hats, they've lost their way,
'Time for dinner!' they chime, then sway.

As night falls, the moon's in a hat,
Casting giggles over the shore, imagine that!
Dreams sail across the shimmering sea,
Where the silliness flows, wild and free.

## Watercolor Skies

Clouds flutter like butterflies bold,
Painting sunsets in purple and gold.
A seagull squawks, 'What a view!'
As a kid begs for one more ice cream scoop too.

The beach ball bounces with a loud 'pop!',
Children chasing it, never want to stop.
A sandcastle rises, then starts to lean,
'There's a moat!' shouts one, 'with fishies unseen!'

The tide giggles as it tickles toes,
While a seaweed wig makes everyone pose.
The sun wearing shades, so cool and bright,
Winks at the surfers with sheer delight.

And as the day turns to nighttime glory,
The stars get ready to tell their story.
In a world where humor blends with the sky,
Every glance up makes the spirit fly.

## Sailing into Imagination

A boat made of candy floats with ease,
While pirates munch on waffles and cheese.
Their treasure map, a pastry delight,
Leads to donuts shining under moonlight.

Smelly fish pull pranks on the crew,
While rain clouds look angry—oh, what to do?
They fling jellybeans, causing a splash,
As sailors slip and slide in a crash.

The octopus plays the ukulele bright,
While singing songs that tickle with light.
Mermaids knit with yarn from shipwrecked dreams,
Creating funny hats with outrageous themes.

As they sail into the unknown, oh my,
Adventure awaits under a giggly sky.
Each wave whispers secrets, each breeze a laugh,
In this land of dreams that will never end half.

## Journeys in the Surf

A seagull perched with a snack so sweet,
It stole my sandwich, oh what a feat!
Then chased by waves that crash and spin,
I waved goodbye, and it wore a grin.

With rubber ducks floating, we sailed quite far,
Chasing the sun in our beachside car.
The surfboards giggled as they tumbled down,
Each somersault earned its own sandy crown.

We danced with crabs, they said we were cool,
Their sideways shuffle made us look like fools.
But laughter echoed through salty air,
In this wonder-filled place without a care.

As dusk approached with a glowing hue,
We painted the waves in a rainbow too.
Our goofy antics danced with the tide,
Oh, what a journey, laughter as our guide!

**The Pulse of the Ocean**

When I dipped my toes, who knew it would bite?
A clam found dinner and held on tight!
I squealed, it laughed, we played this game,
The ocean's pulse, forever the same.

There's a fish with glasses, it swam in style,
Offering fashion tips with a fishy smile.
It told me to twirl, to stop, and to prance,
Provoking an awkward ocean-side dance.

And whales that sang in a wobbly tune,
Pulled me in close like a friendly balloon.
We laughed 'til we cried, my fishy mates,
In this melody of joy, how time, it waits!

With waves that wink at the sand-splashed feet,
We pirouetted and tangled in salty beat.
The world felt light, all worries afloat,
As giggles drifted on the crest of a boat.

## Luminous Shores

At night when the stars dip into the sea,
The crabs in tuxedos dance wild and free.
With shells as their hats, they twirl and they spin,
This beach bash party was truly a win!

The glow of the sand made it hard to tell,
If the magic was there, or just a bright shell.
A jellyfish led with its glowing light,
While seagulls grooved, what a whimsical sight!

A starfish clapped hands with eight limbs so spry,
Said, "Join in the fun, you're way too shy!"
We laughed till the sand got stuck in our hair,
With silly sea creatures beyond compare.

When morning came knocking with bright sunny rays,
We left them behind in our star-studded plays.
But that glow of the night kept the smiles in store,
For laughter shared 'neath the skies we adore.

## Beyond the Coral Gates

Beneath coral arches, a party was set,
With fish wearing hats, it was quite the bet.
The octopus served drinks in a shiny shell,
And told tall tales that we knew all too well!

A dolphin arrived, with a flip and a squeal,
Said, "Dance with me now, let's make a big deal!"
With wiggly moves that made everyone laugh,
We slid on the waves like we were on a raft.

Then came a turtle, slow as can be,
Said, "Life's a race, just take it from me."
As we zoomed past, he chuckled with glee,
It's not about speed; it's about being free!

With bubbles of joy floating all around,
We twirled and we twinked, never fell to the ground.
The gates of the sea held secrets, it's true,
But the laughter we shared stole the spotlight too!

## **Currents of Thoughtful Reverie**

A fish in a suit went to the ball,
Twirled on the dance floor, but took a fall.
His friends gave a laugh, they couldn't believe,
That swimming with style's a tricky reprieve.

Jellyfish juggle, what a sight to see,
They float and they flounder with such glee.
Octopus judges, a critter so wise,
But nope, that last flip was not a surprise!

Seagulls are snooty, with sandwiches bold,
They squawk and they laugh, oh, behold!
While crabs clap their claws in a rhythm so sweet,
Dancing along to the tide's witty beat.

Mermaids in glasses discuss the best kind,
Of seaweed salad, oh, aren't they refined?
Starlit discussions on currents and waves,
In the ocean of jokes, we're all a bit dazed.

## The Call of Distant Shores

A pelican lands with a plop and a splash,
Trying to fit in, but oh what a crash!
Her beak's full of snacks that she saved from her flight,
She joins in the fun, what a comical sight!

The waves are a chorus of giggles and taps,
As crabs build their castles and slip through the gaps.
Starfish wear hats made of kelp and of foam,
In the land of the wavy, all critters feel home.

Dolphins do flips, creating a show,
While fish in tuxedos cheer them below.
The sun starts to set, a comedic parade,
As waves churn with laughter, no need to evade.

Seashells whisper secrets of jocular tales,
Of pirates who tripped on their own rubber sails.
At night, when the stars paint the ocean with light,
The laughter echoes on through the whimsical night.

## Murmurs of the Salted Breeze

A crab and a clam once had a debate,
On who'd make better friends for their fate.
With pincers a-clattering and shells all aglow,
They giggled and sparred, oh, the salt did flow!

Seagulls provide commentary like witty prose,
As fish play charades with a wink of their nose.
A dolphin nearby shimmies and sways,
His moves leave us laughing for days upon days.

The breeze carries whispers of silly old myths,
Like prawns who can tango with rhythm and riffs.
Each bubble that pops brings a chuckle so light,
In the playful embrace of the shimmering night.

As kelp waves in sultry, giggly delight,
Creatures conspire in the glow of the night.
With laughter as salty as the sea foam's crest,
They share in the joy that this world has expressed.

**Ripples in the Space Between**

A whale in a tutu dances with flair,
He twirls through the water, without a care.
Fish form a conga, oh what a sight,
In the deep blue disco, they dance through the night!

The shells keep time with a rhythmic clap,
As crabs form a line, a hilarious map.
With each silly step, they create such delight,
That even the seaweed begins to ignite!

Starlights reflect on this stage of the sea,
As giggles erupt from each corner, you see.
The currents all churn with laughter and jest,
In the splashy confetti of bubbly finesse.

So let's raise a tide to this wacky soirée,
Where water and laughter blend in a play.
In ripples of fun, we'll sway and we'll sing,
A celebration of joy that the ocean will bring!

## Kaleidoscope of Ambers and Ash

In the wood where shadows play,
Squirrels throw a wild ballet.
Jumping over mounds of leaves,
While the trees giggle and tease.

A fox in orange, quite a sight,
Wears a hat that's far too tight.
He struts around, with utmost pride,
As wandering birds laugh and chide.

Around the fire, where embers glow,
Marshmallows dance and curl just so.
They tell tales of the moon's big grin,
While ants conspire to pop right in.

With giggles shared by all who stop,
The twilight air is quite the hop.
In this place of amber's cheer,
Laughter fades, yet draws us near.

## A Voyage Through Liquid Dreams

On boats of bananas, off we glide,
Sailors shouting, 'Let's take a ride!'
The ocean's waves, a jolly crew,
Chuckling as they chase the blue.

Fish wear glasses, wise as owls,
Reciting poems and cracking howls.
Octopuses juggle seashells bright,
While seagulls sing a tune of flight.

We dive through currents, slippery and sleek,
Where jellybeans bounce and dolphins peek.
Underwater laughter fills the sea,
As treasure chests shout, "Find me, whee!"

In dreams we sail on candy tides,
Waving to hippos in cloud-like rides.
All aboard this wacky stream,
Where whimsy flows in twilight's beam.

## Eternal Flickers of Coastal Lights

At dusk by the shore, lights start to twirl,
Shells wink at stars, giving them a whirl.
Crabs don tuxedos, oh what a sight,
While fish throw confetti of shimmering light.

Lighthouses wear hats that wobble and sway,
Shining bright colors for the night's ballet.
The moon, a DJ with beats that enthrall,
Makes even the barnacles dance at the call.

Seagulls in shades, gossiping away,
Trading secrets of the tides' frolic play.
They strut like models on a sandy runway,
Flicking their wings, basking in the spray.

And from the waves, echoes raucous cheer,
As playful dolphins make their way near.
Together we bask in coastal delight,
Where every blink is a burst of light.

## The Allure of Uncharted Waters

In waters deep where rubber ducks roam,
Pirates plunder candy, making it home.
Mermaids giggle, the seaweed their dress,
Throwing wild parties, causing a mess.

A whale in sunglasses, lounging away,
Sips smoothies of seaweed, thinks it's gourmet.
While crabs host karaoke under the moon,
Even the sharks break out into tune.

Bubble parties with fish of all kinds,
Turtles wearing ties, showing off their finds.
Dolphins in bubbling laughter take flight,
As sea cucumbers join in the night.

Adventure awaits in these waters so grand,
With mysteries hidden in seaweed strands.
Let's drift along in this sea of glee,
Where every wave whispers, "Come dance with me!

## A Beneath the Sea

Down where fish dance and bubbles bubble,
Octopuses giggle, oh what a trouble!
Seaweed twirls like a wiggly dance,
Crabs wear hats, in a joyful prance.

Shells whisper secrets, they laugh and tease,
Starfish play poker, if you please!
Jellyfish jiggle as they float on by,
While dolphins tell jokes that make you cry.

A clam once said, 'I'm quite the pearl!'
With friends like these, life's quite a whirl.
Eels share stories of wiggly thrills,
Underwater shenanigans, giving us chills.

Oh, if you dive down, take a good look,
There's humor aplenty in this sea nook!
Where laughter bubbles and joy takes flight,
In a world beneath, ever so bright.

## Stories Carried by the Wind

The wind sings tales, oh what a delight,
Carrying whispers through day and night.
Leaves tell stories of places they've been,
While kites giggle high in skies so keen.

Clouds have a party, with thunderous laughs,
While raindrops dance like playful crafts.
Windsurfers tumble, yell 'Whoosh!' with glee,
As breezy gossip flutters free.

Crows wear sunglasses, oh what a sight,
While squirrels play tag, darting in flight.
The sun snickers as shadows sneak,
In this world, it's humor we seek.

So listen closely, and you might hear,
The wind's funny tales whispering near.
Each chuckle and giggle blows by our way,
Stories that brighten our ordinary day.

## Mermaids' Lament

Mermaids wail of lost treasure and fun,
As they swap fish tales beneath the sun.
Their voices echo through waves of the sea,
While singing of seahorses wishing to flee.

One mermaid lost her very best hat,
Now a crab wears it, how quaint is that?
With shells for instruments, they play out of tune,
Dancing in circles under the moon.

A dolphin chimes in, with a laugh so sly,
'You've lost more than hats, don't be shy!'
Octopus joins with an ink-splattered joke,
And laughter erupts as the sea folks provoke.

So when they lament, don't shed a tear,
For each funny story brings laughter near.
With pranks and with jests, they swim through their plight,
Creating a symphony of joy and light.

**Shores of Imagination**

On the sandy shores where dreams take a stroll,
Seagulls wear sunglasses, oh, what a goal!
Children build castles with giggles and sand,
While waves tickle toes, oh isn't it grand?

A crab in a tux walks with such flair,
'Today's a big day, I'm off to a fair!'
The tide brings in nonsense, a treasure so vast,
As clams swap tales of their glorious past.

Kites zoom overhead like they're late for a feast,
While hermit crabs dance, with moves quite the beast.
The tide pools are laughing, reflecting the skies,
With sparkle and humor, they bring such surprise.

So come to the shores where fun meets the sand,
With each wave of laughter, lend a hand.
In this realm of magic, let your heart sway,
For joy paints our world in the brightest way.

## **Glimpses of Infinity**

In a world of socks and shoes,
A penguin slips, what a ruse!
He skates across the melting ice,
Laughing fish shout, "This is nice!"

Upon a cloud, the cows take flight,
Discussing stars and pizza night.
One says, "Why don't we moo in tune?"
The moon bops along to their cartoon!

A jellybean boat sets sail,
With gummy bears telling a tale.
They laugh and dance, so full of cheer,
Who knew a shark could yodel here?

Through candy hills, the raindrops fall,
Lollipops giggle, not shy at all.
With every splash, the world spins wild,
Bring out the soap, we're soap-bubble styled!

## Kaleidoscope of the Horizon

At sunrise, the bananas sing,
As flamingos do their spring fling.
A crayon sky, all swirls of hue,
And goofy squirrels dance in view.

The jellyfish throw a beach bash,
With seashells wearing sunglasses.
Each wave's a giggle, a playful tease,
As clams and crabs shake legs with ease.

Cartwheeling dolphins hop on by,
Who knew a fish could dance so high?
With guppies forming a human train,
Sailing on spaghetti made from rain!

The sun wearing shades calls, "Let's play!"
As umbrella birds just sway and sway.
With every squawk, a new joke starts,
This wild horizon warms our hearts!

## A Voyage of Discovery

On a snail-ship, slow and steady,
With pickle sails all bright and ready.
We chart the course through jelly seas,
Dodging giggles and humming bees.

An octopus serves our lunch buffet,
With twisty straws and lemon spray.
Each sip a bubble, full of cheer,
Makes us whistle, then disappear!

To the island made of marshmallow,
Where crickets play an upbeat cello.
The coconut tree plays peek-a-boo,
And coconuts dance just for you.

As night arrives, glowworms glow,
In jello boats, we all row slow.
The stars tell tales of funny sights,
And we laugh till dawn and hold on tight!

**Celestial Currents**

The fish all wear their party hats,
As jellybeans swim with acrobats,
The stars are sipping minty tea,
While singing whales juggle with glee.

The ocean dreams in wobbly hues,
As crabs gossip in fancy shoes,
The dolphins dance a silly jig,
While oysters plan their next big gig.

Bright sea urchins throw confetti,
While octopuses get all sweaty,
The seaweed sways to a bouncy beat,
As the tide rolls in with pirouette feet.

So come and join this seaside ball,
Where the laughter echoes, the sea does call,
In this whirlpool of absurd delight,
We'll dance until we see the light.

**Chasing the Horizon**

A crab with dreams of flight so grand,
Built a tiny rocket out of sand,
He aimed for clouds, just a little shy,
But slipped on seashells and said, 'Oh my!'

The gulls all cackled, 'Nice try, old chap!'
As he flopped and tumbled in his cap,
He skittered sideways, grabbed a star,
Injected it into his lunchbox car.

To the horizon, laughter echoes far,
With jellyfish driving a jelly jar,
They zoom and loop, what a silly sight,
Chasing daylight, ignoring the night.

But waves just giggle, watching the scene,
While squids throw confetti, bright and keen,
So onward, dear crab, don't lose your spark,
Adventure awaits beyond the park!

## **Moonlit Reflections**

A clam kicked back, the moon's bright ray,
He heard the tide say, 'What a great day!'
Starfish basked in moonbeam pools,
While shrimps played tunes using soda cans as tools.

The silver waves made faces, oh dear,
As sea cucumbers rolled from gear to gear,
They giggled and bubbled, 'Let's dine a bit!'
On plankton pie and sea-foam grit.

With reflections dancing, care free and spry,
The moon smiled warmly at napping fish nearby,
'Let's throw a fiesta right here,' they said,
While plankton brought chips—well, that's widespread!

So come find your glow in this oceanic plight,
Where laughter's abundant in the silvery light,
In a world where silliness swims and basks,
Let's join the party, that's all we ask!

## The Dance of Waves

On a beach where the wind plays the flute,
The waves tap dance in bubblegum boots,
They twisted and twirled in a grand ballet,
As sandcastles cheered, 'Hip, hip, hooray!'

Starfish threw shells like confetti from the sky,
While sea turtles honked, 'We're flying high!'
A parade of crabs strutted by the shore,
Waving their claws, 'Who needs to score?'

The surf rode high, doing loop-de-loops,
While dancing anemones formed little groups,
The sun dipped low, casting a warm glow,
As the sea giggled, 'Come join the show!'

In the splash and the sparkle, let laughter stay,
With each little wave shall we waltz and sway,
For in this ocean, humor rides the crest,
Join the dance, and you'll feel truly blessed!

## **Beneath the Velvet Sky**

Beneath a starry quilt so bright,
A crab danced wildly in delight.
It tried to impress a passing shrimp,
But slipped and gave the beach a limp.

The seagulls squawked with laughter loud,
As waves rolled in to form a crowd.
The moon winked down, a playful sight,
While beach balls soared into the night.

## **Rhythms of the Surf**

Waves crash down with a splish and splash,
On sandy shores they make a dash.
A dolphin sneezes, gives a cheer,
As kids build castles from their beer.

With every swell comes a new surprise,
A floating tire gives crabs a rise.
They dance and shimmy, oh what a scene,
Amidst the surf, all is serene.

## A Journey Homeward

A seagull rode the breeze so free,
Chasing popcorn tossed from a spree.
He dove and swooped, oh what a sight,
Then missed the catch and took a flight.

A turtle too, slow yet steady,
Snagged a flip-flop, thought it ready.
He wore it like a fancy shoe,
While ocean critters laughed anew.

## Harmony in the Currents

In waters where the seaweed sways,
A school of fish just loves to play.
They twirl and swirl in fishy glee,
While jellyfish float by with esprit.

A clam with style, so keen and bright,
Wears a coral hat, quite the sight.
He strutted by, a true front-runner,
Then tripped on sand—oh, such a stunner!

## A Haven Amongst the Glistening Foam


In a realm where the sea meets the shore,
Lies a crab holding court, no less, no more.
With a crown made of seaweed, he struts with flair,
While fish pass by, pretending not to care.

A seagull swoops down, eyeing a fry,
But the crab simply shouts, 'You won't even try!'
With waves crashing laughter, the sea's on a roll,
And the jellyfish jiggles, that silly old soul.

Barnacles gossip on a rock near the sand,
Saying, 'Did you hear? A starfish's been banned!'
For stealing the show at the sandcastle fair,
Now he's sunbathing, sprawled without a care.

So join in the fun, where the sea's in a spin,
Where laughter's the treasure that bubbles within.
In this haven of splendor, oh, bring all your dreams,
For the ocean's a canvas, with giggles and gleams.

## Mystique of the Unseen Underworld

Down where the clam makes its secretive lair,
Lives a fish that wears glasses, too cool to be rare.
He reads underwater news, much to his delight,
While the shrimp play charades, with shells shining bright.

A squid in a top hat, quite dapper, you see,
Tries to juggle some shells, but drops two on a spree.
The octopus chuckles, changing colors with glee,
Dancing underwater—oh, what a sight to be!

The seaweed sways gently, a curtain of green,
As crabs argue loudly 'bout who is the queen.
With laughter and whispers from creatures in flow,
The underworld blossoms, a carnival show.

So dive into the depths, where absurdities reign,
In the mystique of shadows, there's giggles—not pain.
The secrets they keep are as silly as they,
In the whispers of currents, come join in the play.

## Ebbing Dreams

As the sun dips low, in a sky of soft hues,
A fish starts to muse, with its colorful shoes.
It dreams of a land where the bubbles all sing,
And the sea turtles disco, oh, what fun they bring!

But wait, here comes trouble—an eel with a grin,
"Let's race to the cave, I'm sure I can win!"
The fish takes a challenge, and soon they are gone,
Leaving behind a rumble, the fun's just begun!

A starfish looks on, in a twist of its fate,
Wondering if it's time to dance or to wait.
With a wave of one arm, it beckons with style,
And soon every shell joins in, ready to smile.

So let the tide pull you, the moon starts to beam,
For laughter and joy are the heart of the dream.
In this ebbing of night, as the waves swirl around,
Every flip, every splash, is the best kind of sound.

## Whispers of the Deep

In the depths where the softest whispers collide,
A trio of turtles go for a ride.
They wear little scarves, all matching and neat,
And say, "Look at us! Isn't this pretty sweet?"

A grouper named Gary can't help but complain,
"Why can't you stay still? This movement's insane!"
But the turtles just giggle, and twirl with a spin,
With bubbles of laughter erupting within.

A clownfish joins in, "Let's play hide and seek!"
As the anemone giggles, "I may be a freak!"
With fins flapping fast, they race through the sea,
Every corner a treasure—what fun it would be!

So listen close now, to the stories they weave,
Of laughter and joy in the world they conceive.
In the whispers of currents, there's mischief and play,
In the depths of the ocean, come join in the fray!

## Navigating Enchantment

The fish are wearing fancy hats,
And seagulls sing in jazzy chats.
A crab's got skills, he does a dance,
While jellyfish float in a wobbly trance.

The seaweed waves like it's on a spree,
Shells are playing hide and seek with glee.
A starfish told a joke so sly,
All the blennies laughed and waved goodbye.

Sandy beaches hold a treasure trove,
A lost rubber duck, oh what a grove!
The waves crash in like a ticklish tease,
Seashells giggle in the salty breeze.

With every splash, a joyful cheer,
Even the dolphins are sipping beer!
The ocean's full of whimsy and fun,
Join the party, everyone!

## Distant Echoes of the Deep

Whales are crooning in a silly tone,
Mermaids are knitting by the coral throne.
A shipwrecked pirate lost his shoe,
He's rockin' an octopus for a crew!

Squids are darting in a paintball fight,
While orcas dance under the moonlight.
A crab with sunglasses walks the line,
He's got a mystery we can't define!

The banter of waves, a comic relief,
As lobsters crack jokes beyond belief.
A school of fish, they giggle and flip,
"Who needs a boat, when you've got a ship?"

Under the surface, secrets are shared,
Anemones chuckle, never impaired.
In the depths, the humor's profound,
With each bubble, laughter's unbound!

## Shadows Among the Waves

The shadows dance, all sea monsters play,
A dragon's grillin' on a grill made of clay.
A mermaid shrieks, "Make way for the clown!"
As octopuses juggle, never let down!

Sea cucumbers gossip, oh what a sight,
The dolphin tricks are pure delight.
"Moi? A pirate? No, just a fool!"
As fishy friends swim back to school.

A shadow lurks, in a funny way,
It mimics me, come out to play!
With sea stars giggling on the rocks,
The ocean's whispers, those friendly knocks.

Laughter lies just beneath the waves,
Grinning snails and playful braves.
From jellyfish tales to lobster jokes,
In these shadows, joy invokes!

## The Ocean's Lullaby

The ocean hums a gentle tune,
With starfish dancing 'neath the moon.
Seashells echo a comic beret,
As crabs do the cha-cha, hip-hip hooray!

A sleepy shark says, "I'm off to snooze,"
But a pesky wave steals his news.
"Wake up, my friend, the party's begun!"
As starry-eyed fish leap, oh what fun!

The tide's a jokester with a riddle,
Tickling sands like it's playing fiddle.
A moon jelly glows, a mischievous sight,
Playing pranks on the gulls in flight.

With lullabies laced in salty air,
Waves rock the beach without a care.
So laugh along with the ocean's sigh,
In its arms, we're all free to fly!

## Reflections of an Infinite Horizon

A crab in a bowtie slips and slides,
He winks at a seagull who giggles and hides.
The fish wear sunglasses, chilling by the reef,
While the octopus juggles, causing quite a belief.

The clams hold a meeting beneath the blue sea,
Debating if pearls are as shiny as tea.
Starfish have parties, dancing around,
While a turtle spins tales without making a sound.

With dolphins providing a splashy good time,
They sing little verses that almost rhyme.
A seaweed band plays a bouncy tune,
As crabs clap along, strutting under the moon.

In this world of giggles, splashes, and fun,
Each wave brings a joke, and laughter's never done.
The horizon stretches wide, with quirks along the way,
Where the ocean holds secrets for a punchline play.

## The Lullaby of the Ocean's Heart

The fishy serenade starts with a splash,
A lobster in pajamas makes quite the dash.
The waves in their rhythm rock everyone slow,
As clams close their eyes, dreaming 'neath the flow.

An electric eel hums a soothing sound,
While crabs prance in reels on the sandy ground.
Bubbles rise up with giggles and glows,
Each pop makes a laughter that everyone knows.

Jellyfish float by in pajamas of light,
They glow like the stars on a magical night.
A sea turtle snores, wrapped up in a dream,
While otters hold hands in a nighttime theme.

With laughter like waves that roll in then out,
The moon winks at fish, who are dancing about.
In the lullaby's arms, the sea softly sighs,
As the ocean's heart whispers, under bright skies.

## Ebb and Flow of Distant Stars

The stars in the ocean play tag with the moon,
While sea urchins wear shoes, and dance to a tune.
A whale sings a ballad, a soft, silly sound,
Encouraging bubbles to float all around.

As the tide pulls away, crabs scuttle in glee,
Trying on shells that look fancy and free.
Octopus fashion shows, a splash of delight,
With outfits designed in the deep, starry night.

Each wave brings a game of catch me if you can,
Dolphins leap high, performing the plan.
A starfish holds secrets of who wore what best,
While sea cucumbers giggle, feeling quite blessed.

In this cosmic dance of bright laughter and cheer,
Every flicker and splash draws a friend ever near.
The ocean's a stage, with guests from afar,
Crafting stories beneath each shimmering star.

## Serenade of the Swaying Sands

The dunes hold a concert with grains on the rise,
Singing out loud as the wind gently sighs.
A lizard in sunglasses struts on the scene,
While a cactus does yoga, looking serene.

Sandcastles stand proud, but one starts to lean,
As seagulls throw beach balls in moments unseen.
The whispers of grains tickle feet walking by,
While tumbleweeds giggle at clouds passing high.

A hermit crab trots with a shell far too grand,
Waving to breezes that blow through the sand.
With footprints like stories crafted in time,
Every step is a laughter, a soft little rhyme.

In this cheerful space where the sun shines so bright,
The dunes hold a party, dancing till night.
With every soft whisper and twinkle of light,
Life's funny and bright in this sandy delight.

## Shadows Cast by the Surf

The waves dance around, a silly charade,
Crabs in a hurry, see how they parade.
A seagull drops fries in its oceanic quest,
While fish play tag in their finned little jest.

The sun's running late, it trips on a beam,
As starfish crack jokes, trying hard not to dream.
Shells gossip in whispers, with pearls in their tale,
While clams take a nap in their soft, sandy sail.

## The Alchemy of Ocean Depths

Squid wear spectacles, reading up on their fate,
While dolphins debate if they should skate.
A jellyfish wobbles in an elegant dance,
As octopi chuckle, 'Oh, give them a chance!'

Mermaids in libraries, all lost in their books,
Trade gossip with turtles, who relish their looks.
Cause when the tide's out, the humor runs high,
And sea cucumbers laugh 'til they nearly cry.

## Glistening Secrets at Dusk

As twilight stretches its colorful arms,
A crab juggles shells, attracting some charms.
Glowworms are twinkling, what a sight to behold!
While lobsters play poker with fortunes of gold.

The horizon blinks twice, like it's winking at me,
While fish sing a tune of absurdity.
A sailor finds treasure, a sock in the sand,
And laughs with the tide, it was all just unplanned.

## Wanderlust of the Billowing Sea

The boat dreams of drifting while chasing a breeze,
And fishes debate if they swim with such ease.
With gulls as their guides, they make silly plans,
To hitch a wild ride on the backs of sea fans.

Seashells hold secrets of mischief and fate,
As mermen unite to pick out their next mate.
Amidst all the splashes, there's laughter galore,
As crabs strut their stuff on the soft, sandy floor.

## Enchanted Echoes of the Sea

Seashells gossip on the shore,
Crabs dance 'round in sandy lore.
A starfish asked a fish to sing,
But all it got was our old string.

Seaweed wigs on jellyfish,
Their disco moves a silly wish.
The ocean laughs, it's quite the show,
As waves come in with a bubbly glow.

## A Symphony of Salt and Sky

The seagulls squawk a silly tune,
While surfboards ride the tide at noon.
A fish in shades with a funny grin,
Said, "Catch me if you can, my fin!"

With beach balls bouncing, laughs abound,
Sandy toes dance upon the ground.
A crab tries to join in on the beat,
But trips and tumbles, that's his defeat.

## **Dreams Carried on the Breeze**

Kites fill the sky, oh what a sight,
Chasing seagulls is pure delight.
The wind's a prankster, pulls and tugs,
As turtles surf on cozy rugs.

Footprints tell tales of silly fun,
As crabs play tag, each on the run.
With a wink, the breeze swoops low,
And giggles at the sandcastles' glow.

## Mysteries in the Deep Blue

A fish with glasses reads the map,
While dolphins plan a goofy clap.
The octopus juggles shells so bright,
But drops them at the silliest sight.

A treasure chest filled with rubber ducks,
Sends pirates off to share their luck.
With a wink and nod, the sea does sway,
As laughter bubbles, brightening the day.

## **Beyond the Dunes**

Beneath the sun, a crab in tow,
Dancing sideways, stealing the show.
Seagulls cackle, a comical sight,
While sandcastles wobble, a pitiful plight.

Flip-flops flying, they've lost their way,
Chasing giggles, brightening the day.
Waves roll in, wrapping us tight,
As we trip in laughter, what a delight!

## Treasures in the Ether

Clouds above, they're fluffy as can be,
One looks like pizza, who could disagree?
A kite goes soaring, caught in a breeze,
Then tangles in hair, with puzzling ease.

Picnics spread under a radiant sky,
Ants plot a heist, they're all passing by.
Cackles of laughter, we spill lemonade,
As bees join the party, and join the parade!

## The Quest for Lost Shores

Map in hand, we boldly set sail,
To find the land where fun won't fail.
But the compass spins, it leads us astray,
To ice cream mountains, hooray, hooray!

Mermaids giggle, tossing their hair,
As we untangle ropes, filled with despair.
But wait! A dolphin offers a ride,
And off we go, no fear, no pride!

## **Currents of Magic**

Wands made of seashells, casting a spell,
Jellyfish shimmer, like stars they dwell.
With a flick of a wrist, we summon a wave,
And ride on foam, oh, how we crave!

Sandwiches fly, thanks to the tide,
Naps on the beach, we don't try to hide.
A crab steals a snack, what a silly sight,
We laugh till we cry, in pure delight!

## Ripples of Memory

A crab wore a hat, quite grand and tall,
He waved at the fish, who laughed at the ball.
The waves carried whispers of giggles and pranks,
As the seagull juggled, the audience drank.

Shells rolled in rhythm, a dance on the shore,
Each one telling tales of the sea's silly lore.
A dolphin played fetch with an old shoe once lost,
In this world of wonder, we care not the cost.

The tide brought in treasure, a sock and a spoon,
And starfish discussed all while singing a tune.
With laughter like bubbles, the ocean was bright,
A party of critters, a comical sight.

So next time you wander where the sea meets the sand,
Remember the jesters that live in this land.
For laughter is salty, and the waves always call,
To join in the fun—there's enough for us all.

## Secrets of the Endless Blue

A fish wore a tie, quite the stylish thing,
While octopuses danced wearing crowns made of bling.
The whispers of seaweed had riddles and jokes,
As clams shared their wisdom with comedic pokes.

An otter on skates slid down slippery rocks,
While seals in tuxedos played cards with the clocks.
Each drop of the ocean held humor so sly,
Like bubbles that burst with a twinkling eye.

The porpoises traded their puns like fine pearls,
As jellyfish giggled and spun in great swirls.
Nautilus orators brought tales from afar,
Of pirates and treasure and their pet petting zoo star.

So dive in with laughter, it's deep and it's wide,
Embrace every wave, let your worries subside.
The tales of the deep have a tickle and charm,
In this realm of the blue, there's no fear of harm.

## The Enchanted Coast

At dawn on the beach, the sand castles yawn,
As crabs pull their carts in the light of the dawn.
Mermaids made mischief, and seagulls flew high,
While wise old turtles just chuckled nearby.

A sea cucumber played hide-and-seek very well,
And seaweed gave riddles that no one could tell.
With lighthouses twinkling, like stars in the day,
The coast spun with laughter in its own spry way.

The boats bobbed gently, a choir of glee,
While fish threw a party for the whole ocean spree.
A clam cracked a joke that was "pear"ly unique,
As laughter erupted in a bubbly peak.

So wander the shore where the seashells do chime,
The magic of laughter is truly sublime.
With every wave's splash, let giggles resound,
In the enchanted coast, pure fun can be found.

## Echoes of the Sea

In the depths of the deep where the echoes reside,
A whale told a tale that made all fish glide.
With a splash and a flip, laughter erupted,
As sea urchins joked, their barbs all corrupted.

The waves carried whispers from shrimp on parade,
Who wore tiny hats, looking quite well-made.
Coral reefs chuckled, and bubbles would tease,
As sea stars played chess in a cool ocean breeze.

The sand soaked in stories that tickled the night,
With stories of plankton taking flight.
As the sun set low, painting skies with a grin,
The sea held its secrets, let the fun begin!

So listen for laughter when tide pools invite,
To the symphony of joy where the sea holds you tight.
With sounds of the ocean, come dance and play near,
In echoes of whims that bring warmth and cheer.

www.ingramcontent.com/pod-product-compliance
Lightning Source LLC
Chambersburg PA
CBHW060138230426
43661CB00003B/480